CHINESE NEW YEAR

written by
Dwayne Douglas Kohn

Smart As A Fox Teaching Materials are available from your local teacher supply store or purchase online at: www.MisterKindergarten.com. For materials in Spanish, please visit: www.PrimerGrado.com. We publish over 100 titles in a variety of languages.

SMART AS A FOX
BOX 4334
OCEANSIDE, CALIFORNIA
92052-4334

©2012 Smart As A Fox

CHINES

MW01131609

New Year, or the "Spring Festival" as it is known in China, is the longest and most important holiday in China. The new year begins on the first day of the first month according to their lunar calendar, which means the dates change from year to year since dates in the lunar calendar and the Western solar calendar do not align. The New Year's festivities end two weeks later on the 15th day of the first month on what is known as the Lantern Festival.

In China years are divided into cycles of 12. Each year is named after an animal. We have included a version of a well-known story that explains how the animals were chosen, along with flash cards that may be used to illustrate the story as it is told.

The western and Chinese zodiacs both contain 12 signs. However, whereas the western zodiac has one symbol per month, the Chinese zodiac represents an entire year. It is believed that a person displays the characteristics of the animal of the year in which they were born.

During the Chinese New Year's celebrations, there are many traditional activities, some local and others celebrated universally. The Chinese believe that as they enter a new year, they should start a new beginning. They clean their houses, pay off all of their debts, purchase new clothes, paint their doors, and even get new haircuts in order to have a fresh start for the new year.

Homes throughout China are decorated with special banners, many of which are red and gold; the traditional representations of happiness and prosperity. We have included these bright banners to decorate your classroom for the new year.

One very fun tradition of the Chinese New Year is exchanging gifts. A traditional present that is given is small red envelopes filled with "lucky money". These envelopes are given to children by their family and friends. Your students can make their own red envelope and even fill it with "Chinese money!"

The dragon is a very popular symbol for the Chinese New Year. It is a symbol of strength and good luck. A Chinese New Year celebration would not be complete without a giant dragon parading down the street. The dragon costume is always very colorful and can be up to 100 feet long. People inside the costume make the dragon move up and down as it zigzags past the spectators. Your students can make their very own dragon! They can make a dragon mask, a dragon paper bag puppet, a fan-folded paper dragon or even write a story on dragon-shaped writing paper. (Run the stationery off on card stock and glue popsicle sticks to the first and third sections of the dragon to make it move like in the parade!)

During the Chinese New Year you will see fireworks and hear firecrackers! There are many beliefs about why fireworks are used. One belief is that the noise of the fireworks is supposed to scare away all evil spirits allowing the new year to begin without misfortunes. Your students will love making the pretend firecracker that we have provided.

Other activities that will help in your Chinese New Year celebration include figurines that feature traditional Chinese clothing, a book cover for creating a writing book, and paper cut art to decorate the classroom.

This unit contains many activities that can be used any time during the year in a study of the country and customs of China. There is a map of China, a Chinese flag, a traditional hat (that the students can actually wear!), a paper figure that holds their compositions, a model of the Forbidden City, traditional Chinese lanterns and so much more!

If that weren't enough, there are also many projects that actually teach the Chinese language! Your students will be counting to ten in no time and naming the colors of the rainbow in Chinese with the included flip booklets!

Gong Xi Fa Cai!
Happy New Year!

RAT | OX | TIGER | RABBIT

THE CHINESE ZODIAC

There are several stories about how the animals were chosen for the Chinese zodiac. This is one of the most popular. While you are telling this story to your students, you may wish to use the animal flash cards included with this unit. Have the students cut them apart, hold up the animals as you mention them in the story, and put them in the order that they finished the race.

Long, long ago in China, the Emperor decided that each year should be named after a different animal. An announcement was made to all of the animals of the land that there would be a race. The animals would have to cross a fast flowing river. The first 12 across would each have a year of the zodiac named after them.

All of the animals lined up along the river bank. The rat and the cat, who were so small, began to complain that it wasn't fair that they had to race against such big animals. A kind-hearted ox standing next to them offered to carry them across the river on his back. The rat and the cat quickly jumped up and were very happy when the ox soon took the lead in the race. They had almost reached the other bank when the rat suddenly turned and pushed the cat into the river. The cat, who was not a very good swimmer, struggled just to keep his head above water. Then, just before the ox was about to win the race, the rat jumped on head of the ox and landed at the feet of the Emperor to finish first.

"Well done," said the Emperor to the rat. "The first year of the zodiac will be named after you." The poor ox had been tricked into second place and the second year of the zodiac was named after him.

Shortly afterwards, the tiger emerged from the water to claim third place. Next to arrive was the rabbit, who hadn't swum across at all. He had hopped across on the backs of the other animals! "The third year will be known as 'The Year of the Tiger' and the fourth year will now be the 'Year of the Rabbit!'" said the Emperor.

Suddenly, a dragon swooped down from the sky to take fifth place. The Emperor looked at the dragon and asked, "You can fly so quickly. Why weren't you the first to win?"

The dragon stepped forward and said, "I live high up in the mountains. I just now heard that there was to be a race."

"Even with a late start, you still were able to finish well." said the Emperor. "From now on, the fifth year will now be known as 'The Year of the Dragon.'"

The Emperor turned back to the river to see the horse arriving to the bank. But just as the horse was about to exit the river, a snake slithered under the horse, causing the horse to jump back. The snake then became the sixth to finish the race. The horse was not too upset. He still was able to finish seventh.

A few minutes went by and then a log washed ashore carrying a goat, a monkey and a rooster. They explained that they couldn't swim very well and that the monkey had the great idea to float across on a log. The Emperor said the goat would be the eighth zodiac animal, the monkey the ninth and the rooster the tenth.

Now there were only two more positions still available. Who would be the next one across? All eyes were on the river as a dog leapt out of the waves.

"Why are you so late when you are one of the best swimmers?" asked the Emperor.

"On the way across, I saw a stick and I had to chase it. Then there was another stick and I had to chase it too," the dog said, a bit embarrassed.

"Who would be throwing sticks during a race?" asked the Emperor. The monkey looked down and tried to hide.

"Well at least you finished in time to have a year named after you. 'The Year of the Dog' shall be the eleventh year."

There was just one more spot in the zodiac left. Once again, everyone looked to the river to see who the final animal winner would be.

Slowly and carefully from the water emerged a pig.

"Sorry I'm so late," said the pig. "I was hungry and had to eat something. Then that made me tired and I had to take a nap."

"You still made it just in time," said the Emperor. "The last year of the zodiac will be named after you."

As the animals all cheered, the cat, who had been pushed into the river by the rat, finally crawled out of the water.

"I'm sorry," began the Emperor. "You are just a little too late. We already have our 12 winners. Unfortunately, you are number 13."

The cat was very angry with the rat and ever since then cats have never been friends with rats.

For the rest of the afternoon other animals struggled across the river only to find out that they also were too late. The twelve winning animals all beamed with pride knowing that from that day on the years of the Chinese Zodiac would be named after them.

CREATIVE WRITING ACTIVITY

-Which was the next animal to arrive and why was it so late?

-Which animal would you like to be and why?

-Was it fair that the rat became the first animal of the Chinese zodiac?

Book Cover

Staple to blank paper and cut out to create a book!

www.MisterKindergarten.com

The 12 Animals of the Chinese Zodiac

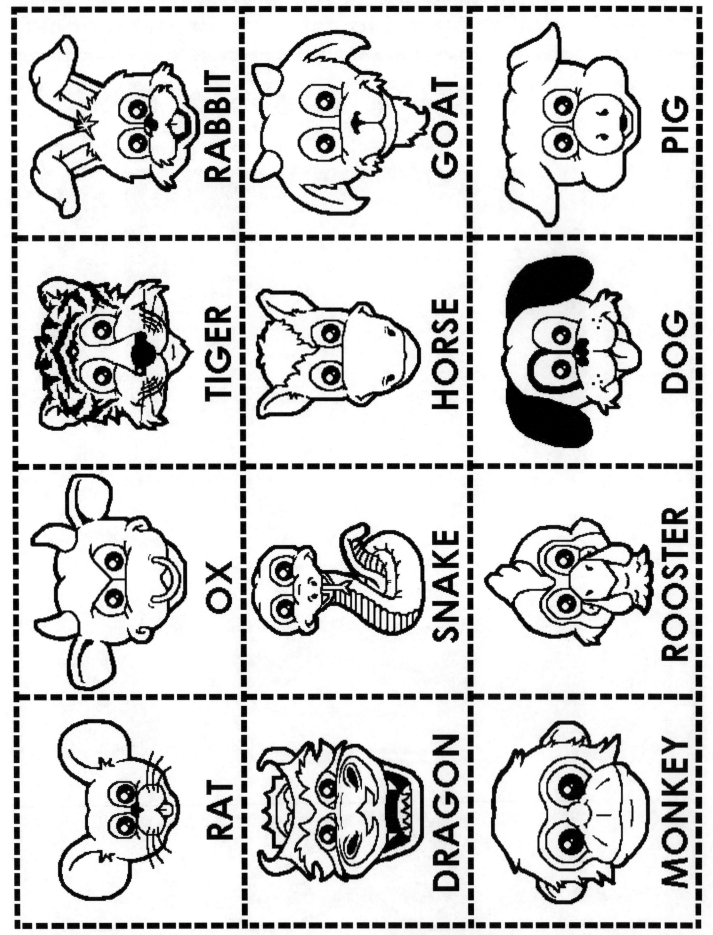

www.MisterKindergarten.com

The 12 Animals of the Chinese Zodiac

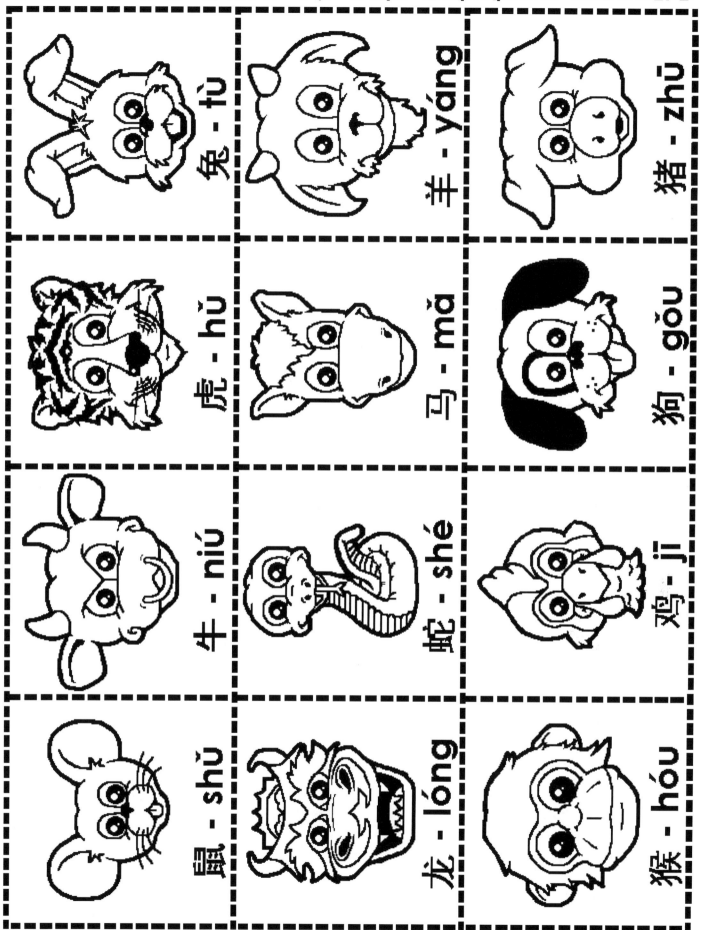

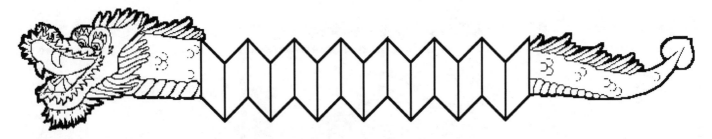

FAN-FOLDED PAPER DRAGON

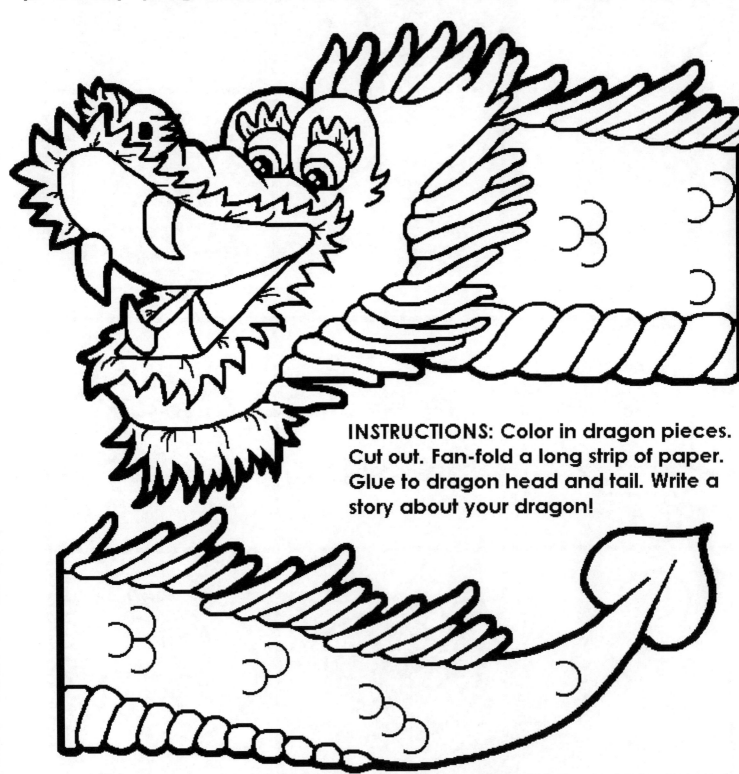

INSTRUCTIONS: Color in dragon pieces. Cut out. Fan-fold a long strip of paper. Glue to dragon head and tail. Write a story about your dragon!

©2012 Dwayne Douglas Kohn   www.MisterKindergarten.com

Chinese Woman

中国女人

Zhōngguó nǚrén

www.MisterKindergarten.com

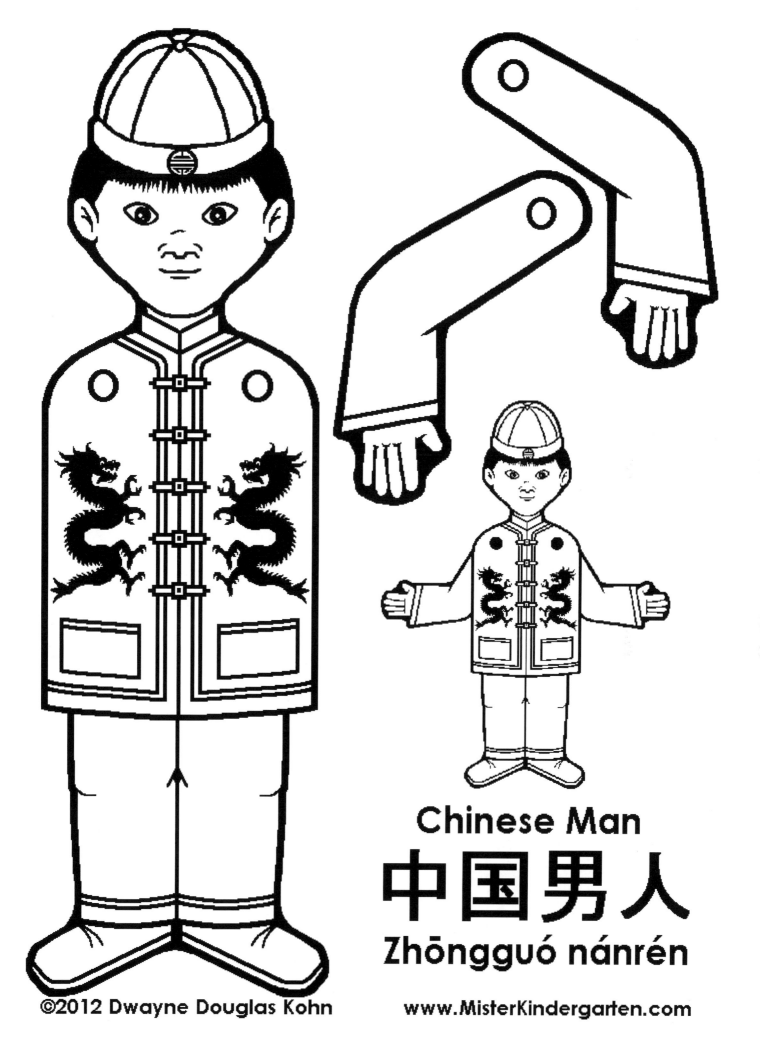

Chinese Man

中国男人

Zhōngguó nánrén

©2012 Dwayne Douglas Kohn

www.MisterKindergarten.com

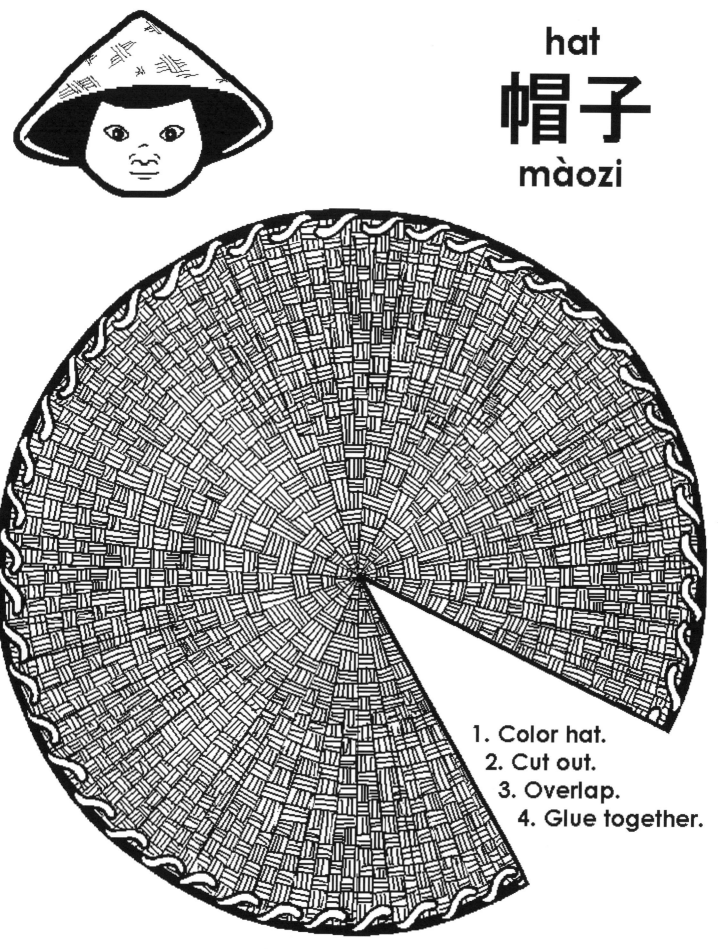

hat

帽子

màozi

1. Color hat.
2. Cut out.
3. Overlap.
4. Glue together.

www.MisterKindergarten.com

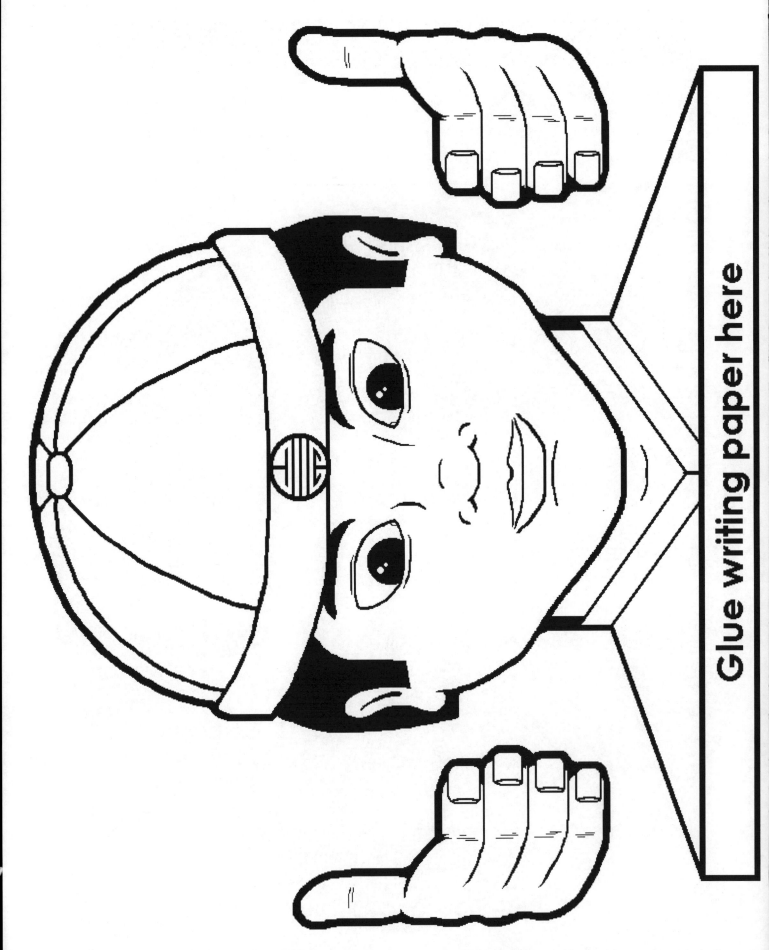

Glue writing paper here

www.MisterKindergarten.com

STORY HOLDER

Glue writing paper here

www.MisterKindergarten.com

THE FORBIDDEN CITY (Gùgōng)

中国新年快乐
中国新年快乐
中国新年快乐
中国新年快乐

www.MisterKindergarten.com

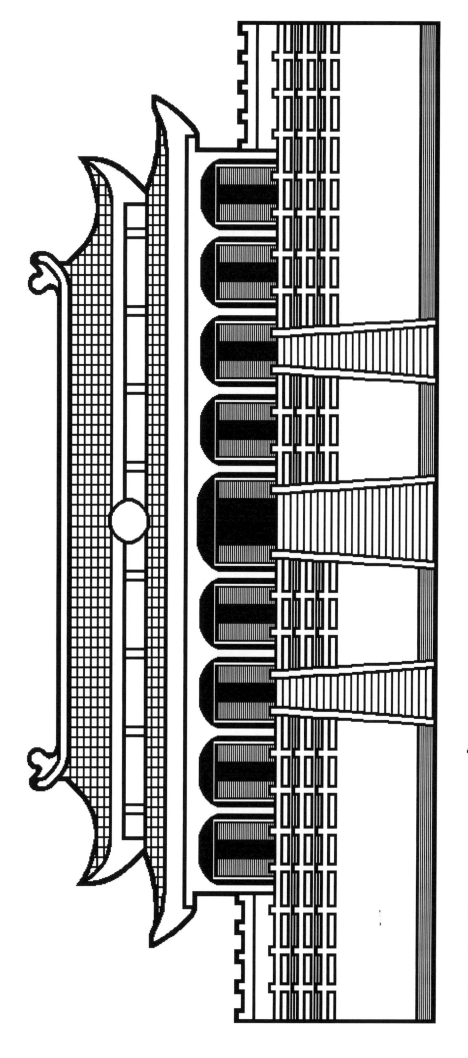

THE FORBIDDEN CITY (back)

THE FORBIDDEN CITY
(sides)

glue to front

glue to front

glue to back

glue to back

Chinese Paper Cut

 www.MisterKindergarten.com

panda   熊猫   xióngmāo

PANDA PUPPET

PAPER PLATE PANDA

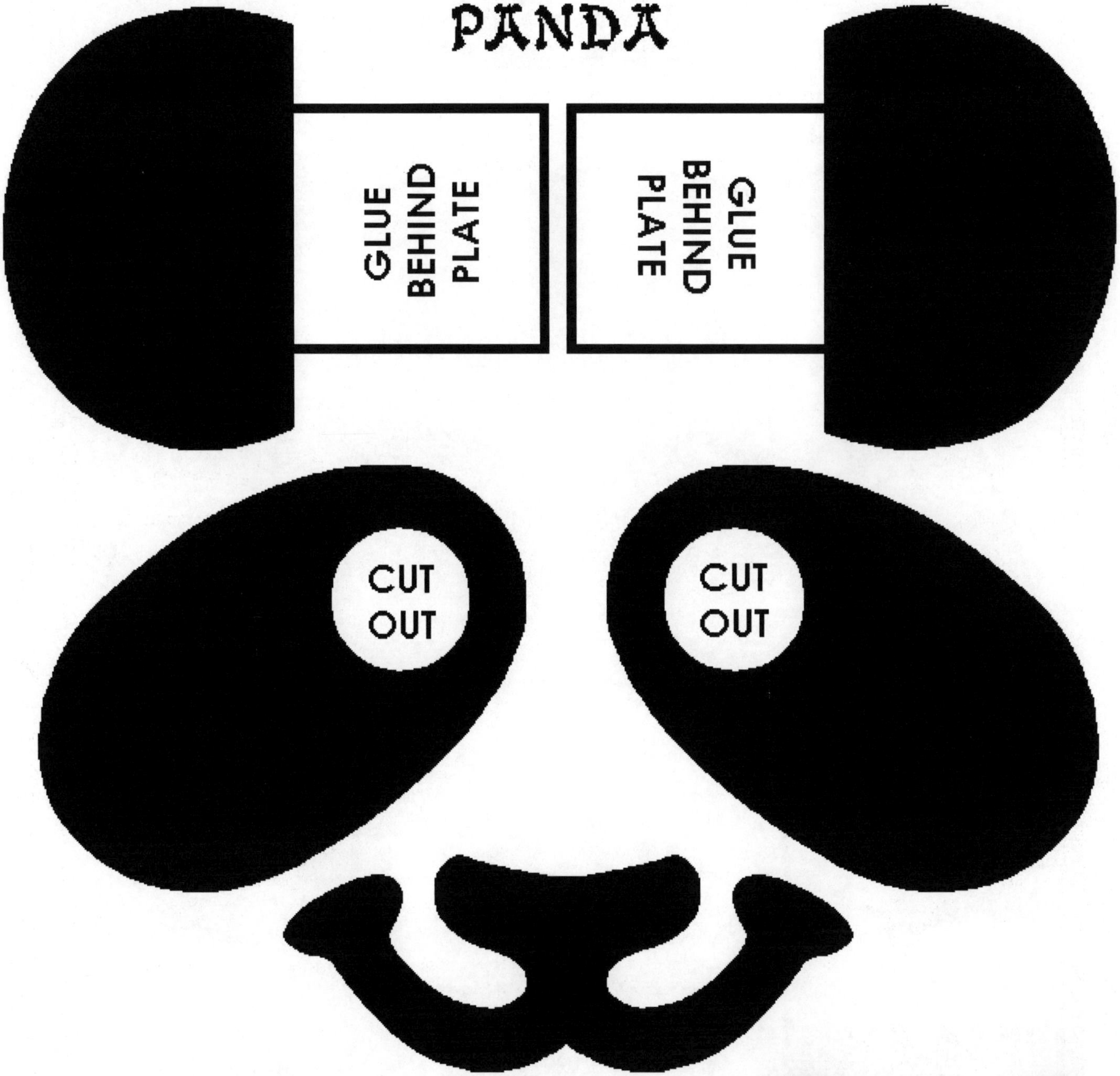

GLUE BEHIND PLATE
GLUE BEHIND PLATE
CUT OUT
CUT OUT

1. Color tongue red.
2. Cut out pieces.
3. Glue to paper plate.
4. Cut out eye holes.
5. Use as a mask.

 www.MisterKindergarten.com

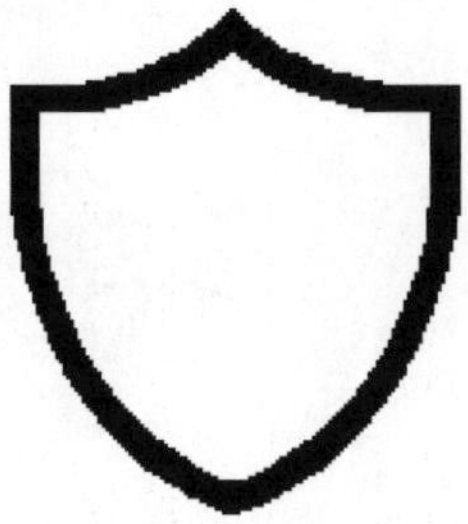

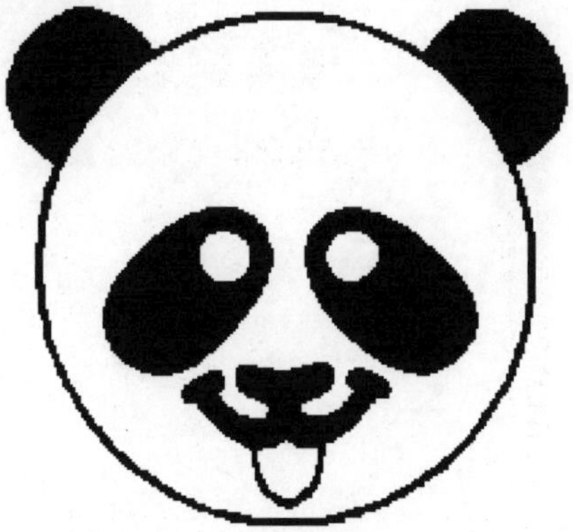

horizontal

vertical

www.MisterKindergarten.com

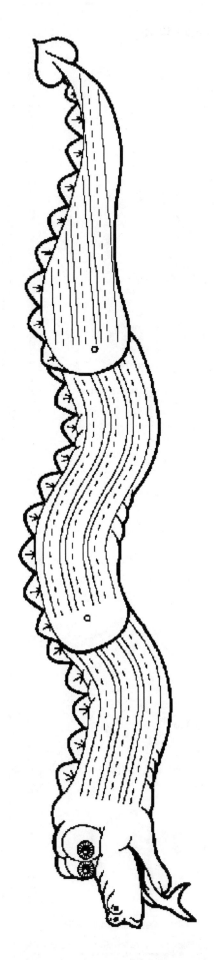

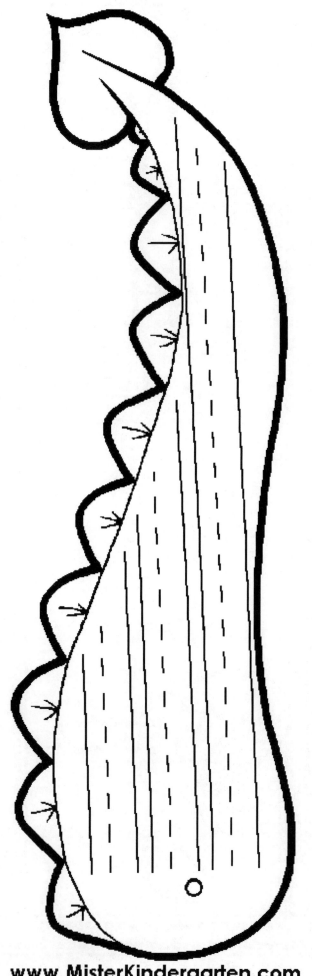

HAPPY CHINESE NEW YEAR!

USE PAPER FASTENERS TO JOIN THE DRAGON BODY PARTS

©2012 Dwayne Douglas Kohn

www.MisterKindergarten.com

Red Envelope

During the Chinese New Year it is traditional for parents to give gifts of "lucky money" to children. The money is always presented in a red envelope. Copy this page on red paper, cut out, fold and glue where indicated to create your own Red Envelope. Use the Chinese bills on the next page to complete your gift!

fold and glue

Happy New Year!

恭喜发财

gōng xǐ fā cái

fold and glue

Cut on solid lines.
Fold on dotted lines.

Tuck in flap - Do not glue.

www.MisterKindergarten.com

Chinese Money

www.MisterKindergarten.com

Map of China

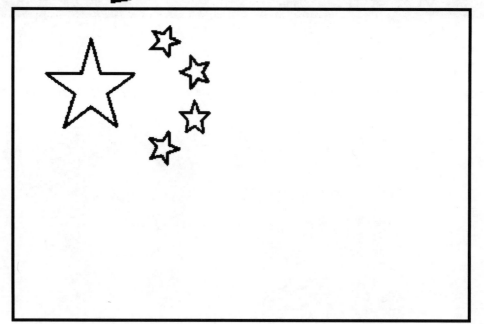

www.MisterKindergarten.com

FLAG OF CHINA

Color the 5 stars yellow and the background red.

www.MisterKindergarten.com

RAINBOW COLORS
IN MANDARIN CHINESE

INSTRUCTIONS:
1. Color pictures the correct color.
2. Carefully cut out pages.
3. Put pages in rainbow order: purple on the bottom, red on top.
4. Put cover (rainbow) on top.
5. Staple pages together on left.

huángsè 黄色

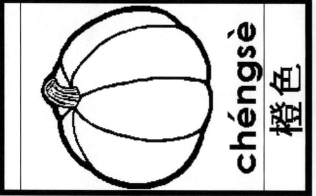

chéngsè 橙色

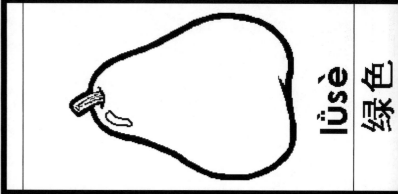

lǜsè 绿色

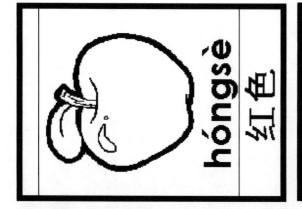

hóngsè 红色

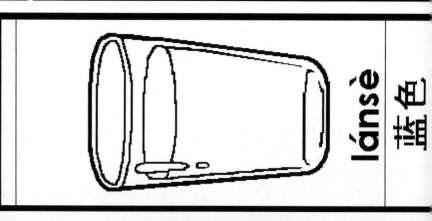

lánsè 蓝色

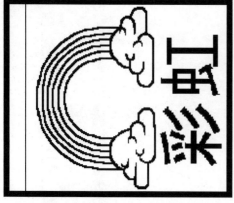

彩虹

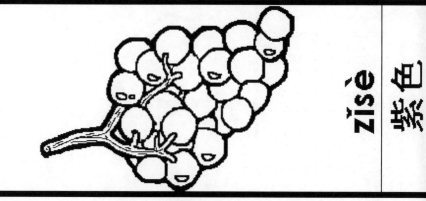

zǐsè 紫色

www.MisterKindergarten.com

一 yī

CHINESE 1-10

INSTRUCTIONS: Color in pages. Carefully cut out pages on thick lines.
Put pages in order. TEN on bottom, ONE on top. Staple on left side.

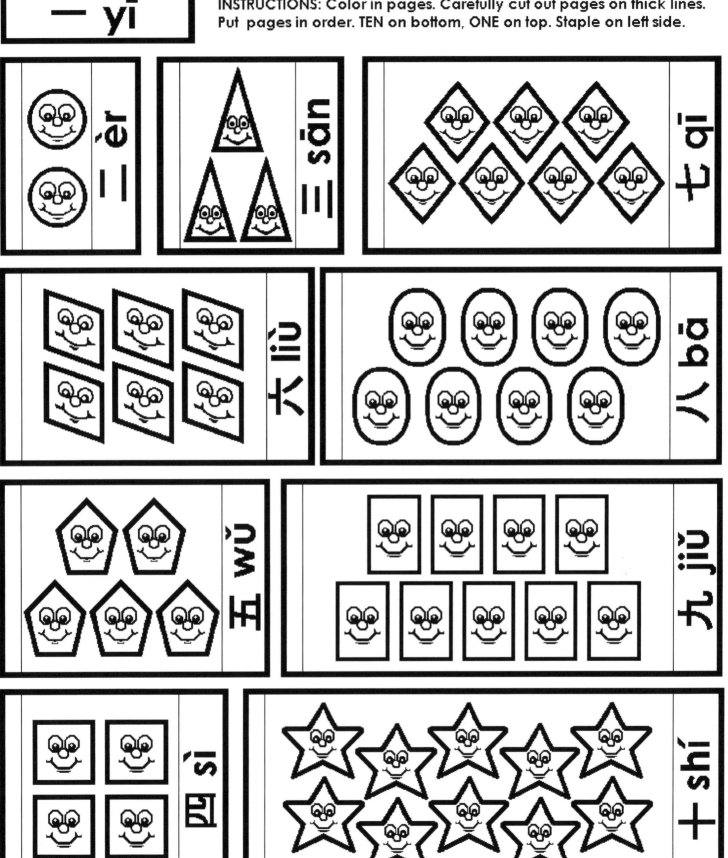

二 èr

三 sān

七 qī

六 liù

八 bā

五 wǔ

九 jiǔ

四 sì

十 shí

www.MisterKindergarten.com

Chinese Lantern

handle

Form a cylinder and glue other end here.

恭賀新禧 Gōnghè xīnxǐ

Happy New Year!

fold in half

Color in the lantern. Cut on the solid lines (rectangle shape). Fold on middle line. Cut on dotted lines.
Open and make into a cylinder. Glue where indicated. Glue the handle inside the top. Hang up.

www.MisterKindergarten.com

firecracker

爆竹

bàozhú

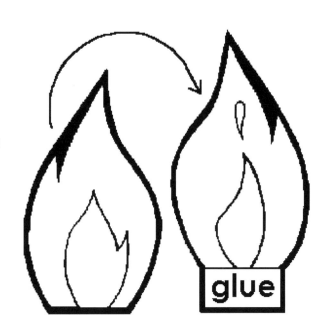

glue

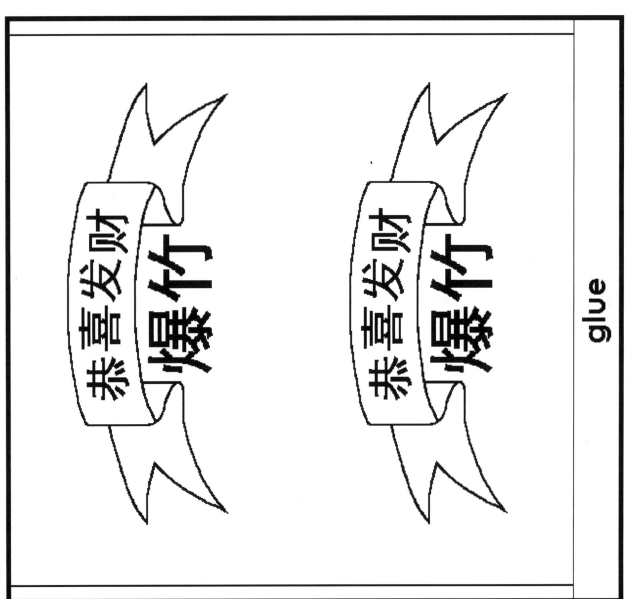

glue

www.MisterKindergarten.com

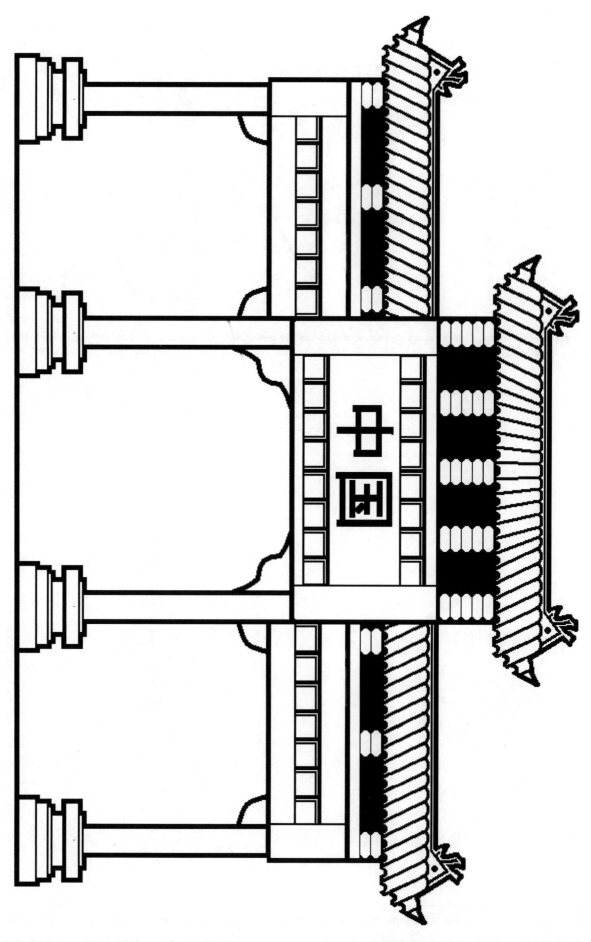

59362220R00020

Made in the USA
Lexington, KY
03 January 2017